50 Leadership Principles PART II:

How to position YOUrself for success

By Jorge Zuazola © founder of American Leadership 17th July 2019

ISBN: 9781081140373

INDEX

PRINCIPLE #51: Become a person of influence through listening

If you can't understand people and work with them, you can't accomplish anything. And you certainly can't become a person of influence. This is truer in the Digital Networking Age. No man would listen to you if he didn't know it was his turn next. Unfortunately, this accurately describes the way too many people approach communication – they're too busy waiting for their turn to really listen to others. God gave us two ears and one mouth and not the other way round.

PRINCIPLE #52: Never digitally criticize anybody personally

There is nothing else that kills the ambitions of a person as criticism from superiors. Never criticize anyone digitally. What do average people do in the Corporate World? The exact opposite. If they don't like a thing, they bawl out their subordinates; if they do like it, they say nothing. As the old couplet says: "Once I did bad and that I heard ever/Twice I did good, but that I heard never". I believe in giving a person incentive to work. People work for recognition because we are all animal spirits and need our spirit to be positive. We need to be in good mental shape to perform digitally.

PRINCIPLE #53: Become a proficient digital reader

Digital Leaders are readers. Reading, like no other single activity, levels the playing field of life, it is the great equalizer. Reading influences us in ways we can't even comprehend. Reading even changes the shape of our brains! Reading transforms us from who we are right now to who we can become in the future. The Avatars in the Digital Network are a first base but when we read inspiring, thought-provoking digital books, we grow richer in all phases of our lives. When we stop to really think about the impact that reading has on our lives, we're left standing in awe, like in the Industrial Age or the 1.0 world.

PRINCIPLE #54: Be a slave to good digital habits

Bad digital habits are the unlocked door to failure. Thus, the first law which you should obey, which precede all others is – *I will form good digital habits and become their slave*. Weak is the digital user who permits his/her thoughts to control his actions; strong is the person who forces his actions to control his/her thoughts. The auto-suggestion even dominates the thoughts that go to the subconscious. All is manageable digitally

PRINCIPLE #55: Set your digital daily goals. a day beforehand

Digital Winners set their digital daily goals the afternoon or evening before. They list on their digital agenda in a priority sequence at least 6 major things to do tomorrow using the urgent-importance planning matrix. The subconscious works overnight on those goals. Therefore, you wake up focused on the task on hand. This applies to both work days and weekends. What gets planned, gets done.

PRINCIPLE #56: Set a 1 million Euro goal to begin your digital wealth career

Some people ask: It is the same being digitally happy than being rich? We usually reply "Yes but it is better to be both rich and digitally happy". Although we have worked very hard for over half a century, we still have done very little. If we do not have 1 Million Dollars/Euros/Pound/Yens at this age, it is our fault.

PRINCIPLE #57: Understand that money is a measure of success

Money is the medium by which earthly success is measured because makes possible the enjoyment of the best the earth affords.

Money is plentiful for those who understand the simple law which governs its acquisition. In the Digital Age money is not even printed in many cases therefore you have to be conscious of your right to be rich.

PRINCIPLE #58: True Digital Financial Freedom

True digital financial freedom is achieved when your pleasure in saving money equals or exceed your pleasure in spending it. This has been always the case even before the books on getting rich were written.
Therefore now with all the digital wealth of knowledge, the avenues of collecting wealth are much wider.

PRINCIPLE #59: Teach money lessons to your children

At what age should you start teaching your children about making money digitally? Most people answer is when your child becomes interested in money but the truth is that even a five-year old child already understands the difference between a five- and a twenty Euro banknote Nowadays you should educate your children at home to walk barefoot with a 5-Euro banknote as sock and put their shoes on. Do it using digital technology until they understand the value of money.

PRINCIPLE #60: Become an investor

One of the biggest differences between employees and digital investors is that these know to cut their losses quickly. Digital investors are not afraid to admit they made a mistake quickly. Digital investors are not into saving face, they are saving money. When they make a bad investment, they cut and run, even if they lose some money. Many non-investors buy an investment and hold on to it all the way down to the bottom which ultimately evaporates in times of financial crisis.

PRINCIPLE #61: Invest wisely in the finance markets

A difficult and serious problem for all investors today is that there is entirely too much free information, hype, promotion, personal information and advice about the stock market. You get it from friends, people at work, the Internet, brokers, stock analysts, advisers, entertaining cable TV and all type of digital media. **It can be very risky and potentially dangerous.** Realistically, there are not too many people you can listen to if you want to avoid confusing, contradictory, and faulty personal opinions. Confine yourself to just a very few LinkediN influencers sources of relevant facts and data and a sound system that has proven to be accurate and profitable over time. Facts are always better than most people's opinion. Opinions do not make money.

PRINCIPLE #62: Have your mind on fire for something worthwhile digitally

The secret is that you have to be on fire for something worth pursuing. When you are pouring yourself out, you never lose energy and vitality in so doing. You only lose energy when life becomes dull in your mind. Your mind is an image maker. Your mind gets bored and therefore tired doing nothing. You don't have to be tired. Get interested in something. Get absolutely enthralled in something. Throw yourself into it with abandon. Get out of yourself. Be somebody. Don't sit around moaning about things, reading the papers, and saying: " Why don't they do something? The man who is out there doing something is not tired. Leadership is action and moving. Digital Leadership clearly shows it in an excellent manner.

PRINCIPLE #63: Be a digital planner

Definiteness of purpose provides context and allows you to put specific digital actions to your overall plans. Drifting, without a goal or purpose, is the first cause of failure: Without a plan for your life, it is easier to follow the course of least resistance, to go with the flow, to drift with the current with no particular destination in mind. Having a definite plan for your plan greatly simplifies the process of making hundreds of daily decisions that affect your ultimate success. When you know where you want to go, you can quickly decide if your actions are moving toward your goal. Without definite precise goals and a plan for their achievement, each decision must be considered in a vacuum because the mind is in mental haze. Goals activate the brain's reticular function.

PRINCIPLE #64: Keep a neat digital appearance

While you should never be obsessed with your looks, you should maintain a neat appearance. When you look good, you feel good. When you feel good, you perform better. If you keep that in mind when you dress in the morning. Before leaving, check the mirror and ask yourself: Am I projecting confidence digitally? Look around your place of residence. Does this appear to be the home of a person with high self-esteem? Many psychiatrists claim a cluttered, unorganized living space is the product of cluttered, unorganized mind. Remove the clutter thus releasing the right mental image. Apply this digitally. Take care of how you present yourself to the digital world.

PRINCIPLE #65: You're your Dreams Firm in a Digital Changing World

Dreaming is like oxygen, you can't live without it. Your brain needs oxygen so your brain needs dreams. People seem to give them up, quicker than anything, for a "reality". Nothing is real as a dream. We are animal spirits with intellect which produces dreams. The world can change around you, but your dream will not. No matter the time. Responsibilities need not erase it. Duties need not obscure it. Because the dream is within you, no one can take it away. Nothing happens unless first a dream. America didn't invent dreaming. But it was the first to make dreaming available to the masses. Now with digital networks the availability is exponential in growth terms.

PRINCIPLE #66: Develop your self-responsibility digital system

Motivation, like adrenaline, tends to work in short spurts. It's like a bath or shower – you need it every day- it simply doesn't last. This is why it's so important to have a self-responsibility digital system – associates, deadlines, prioritized task lists, personal journals, coaches, mentors, leaders, and the like – to keep you accountable and on track. Another key is to be dedicated to continuous improvement. Listening to podcasts, watching youtube on leadership and reading daily from a positive book are keys to your growth. Attend seminars regularly. All this helps you to re-ignite your fire so you can blast through the obstacles more easily.

PRINCIPLE #67: Never lie about your finances

To one extent of another, most people tend to lie about who they are when it comes to their money. Financial lies destroy financial lives. Telling the truth about yourself and your money is the only way to keep what you have and create what you deserve. Do not be a pretender. Be a humble saver and you will succeed digitally. Our 3is (Internet Ideas Incubators) started off with less than a 10 dollars investment which has paid-off very well indeed.

PRINCIPLE #68: Avoid self-deception

Self-deception is a particularly difficult sort of problem. To the extent that organizations are beset with digital self-deception – and most of them are- they cannot see the problem. Most organizations are stuck in the box which has been one of the triggers of the global financial recession of 2009. CRMs are no longer valid. DCSM (Digital Clients Sales Management) are the only option valid.

PRINCIPLE #69: Choose to change and prove it digitally

To blame is much easier than to choose to change. Change or Be Changed: There are two kinds of people – those who are changing and those who are setting themselves up to be victims of change. Unless a crisis actually kills us (often it just feels like it will) it is an opportunity for us to change. And show it digitally to the world. It's a chance to choose a new digital path 4.0 from the industrial path 0.0 because the mind only changes either from an emotional shock or from constant repetition and reprogramming.

PRINCIPLE #70: Use digital teamwork to achieve your dreams

Teamwork makes the dream work. Loyalty alone does not make people candidates for your inner digital circle. But lack of loyalty definitely disqualifies them. Don't keep anyone close to you whom you cannot trust. Victory is preceded by a breakthrough. Breakthroughs make the difference – whether the person is leading or following digitally, famous or obscure, powerful or weak. Successful people do not allow the trivial things in their lives to become important. And conversely, they don't allow the important things to become unimportant. They form a habit of spending their best resources on their best pursuits. They order their activities so that they are always gravitating towards digital success.

PRINCIPLE #71: Be a digital expert in people skills

No matter what your profession is, success in life is primarily about people. If you have good relationships, **life is happy**. Happiness is a state of mind. If there is a conflict or confusion between you and other people, **life is hard**. No amount of money can make you happy if you don't understand people know how to get along with them. Without mastering people skills there is no true success. No matter what type of success you are looking for, people skills are always the foundation of good leadership. That is why you need to be a digital expert to be a leader in the P2P 4.0 Digital Era.

PRINCIPLE #72: Put digital service first

If you put digital service first, money takes care of itself. Humble leadership at all times is the path for ongoing success.

PRINCIPLE #73:Cure psychological malnutrition

The basic, all-important secret to more of the truly good life is to overcome the negative influences of your friends, co-workers, relatives, and others who impact on your dreams and desires. Cure **psychological malnutrition**. This disease, so widespread it goes almost unnoticed, costs the world hundreds of billions of dollars/euros each year. Most people could easily double or triple their incomes by teaching themselves to feed other people psychological nourishment instead of psychological poison. Check every product label when you go to the supermarket to start with. You will learn a lot.

PRINCIPLE #74: Be a decisive digital leader

Decisiveness is your greatest ally as you digitally chart your path through life. Procrastination is a thief, waiting in disguise to rob you of your hopes and dreams. What a cunning word procrastination is. It disguises the real word, castrate, which also means to impoverish or render ineffective. Because you create a mental haze in your mind as opposed to your natural image maker. Do you get the picture? When you procrastinate you are actually impoverishing your future, cutting it off. From now on, every time you go into procrastination mode on digital work, sear this painful image of castration into your mind so that it shocks you into action.

PRINCIPLE #75: Build up digital relationships

You spend approximately 2000 hours a year at your office. Poor work relationships can make even the best job a pain the neck. Positive work relationships can make going to the office a pleasure. Read digitally to learn on how to use the Leadership Touch in your …**Digital Relationships**

.

PRINCIPLE #76: Document your financial statements

I use financial statements that I update at least monthly **which makes all the difference in the world.** This simple management tool allows me to track my money as it comes and goes out. All the guesswork about "Where did your money go?" is gone for good. Yet the 2008 recession has forced me to discipline further and I must do it weekly now.

.

PRINCIPLE #77: Self-manage yourself at least 1 minute

Everybody loses his head 5 minutes a day. The wise person is the one which does not allow these 5 minutes to extend. Make sure that you have handy daily:

One Minute Goals
One Minute Praises
One Minute Reprimands.

That way you can always be in balance internally in your spirit which is your healthy base for success. Looking yourself in the mirror while making affirmations is a sure investment for success.

PRINCIPLE #78:
Understand what America is

The cause of America is in a great measure the cause of all mankind which is necessary to lead the world. Terrorists attacked New York, a symbol of American prosperity to bring us down and the whole world. Yet they did not touch its source. America is successful because of the hard work and creativity and enterprise of the people America's strength, is and always has been, her people.

PRINCIPLE #79: See things from others´ digital viewpoint

Empathy is crucial for your digital success. If there is any one secret of digital success, it lies in the ability to get the another person's point of view and see things from that person's angle as well as from your own, That is so simple, so obvious, that anyone ought to see the truth of it at glance; yet 90 percent of the digital people on this earth ignore it 90 percent of the digital time.

PRINCIPLE #80: Plan for retirement

If you keep doing what you are doing today, which financial level will you exit at age sixty – five?

- Poor $ 55,000 or less per year
- Middle class $ 75,000 to $ 150,000 per year
- Affluent $ 150,000 to $ 1 Million per year
- Rich $ 1 Million or more per year
- Mega Rich $ 1 Million or more a month

It does not make a difference what age you are now when you read this. Simply put a digital plan.

PRINCIPLE #81: Become your own digital cheerleader

Thoughts are things. Every thought has a frequency. To perform at your best, you must become your own digital cheerleader. You must develop a routine of coaching yourself and encouraging yourself to play at the top of your game. Fully **95 percent of your emotions, positive or negative**, are determined by how you to talk to yourself **on a minute-to-minute basis. It is not what happens to you but the way you interpret the things that are happening to you that determines how you feel.** It is your version of events that largely determines whether they motivate or demotivate you, whether they energize or de-energize you. Talk to yourself nicely always on top of your circumstances.

PRINCIPLE #82: Be digitally patient

Patience means showing self-control in the face of adversity. Nine-and-a-half times out of ten, when I worked at a troubled company, the problem was right at the top because management is craft whereas leadership is art. Positionship cannot work well without leadership.

We have become so character-disordered in the Corporate World that the rest of the world is laughing at us! Nobody wants to assume responsibility for anything anymore. Everybody is very impatient. However if you are patient in the digital world, and reasonably consistent, the impatient will look for you to guide them for success.

PRINCIPLE #83: Use your dreams to handle adversity

You MUST dream. Without dreams, we are condemned the status quo. Without dreams, we could never change anything. Dreams motivate us and keep us going. When we face adversity, it is our dreams that hold us together. I specifically list my dreams, when I will achieve them and how they will change my lives.

Dreams are the essential forces in building wealth, strengthening relationships, or creating success. We can motivate other people if we know their dreams. Imagine the power of helping people get what they really want. They will be your friends for life. Very few people have a solid dream. Someone without a dream is unlikely to achieve happiness. Help everyone to build their digital dream.

PRINCIPLE #84: Quitters never win

Qutting is never an option! Time and again the story is the same. The secret to success is simply getting up one more time than you fall down. Whether you are like a solider who was shot down over in wars in the prime of his life or whether you start a new business when everyone else of your age has retired- you, too, can meet the challenges before you actualize your potential and seize a life of abundance. Climb the walls of adversity and build the doors through your challenges until the digital 2.0 world hears your message loud and clear.

PRINCIPLE #85: Drink 3 liters of water a day

Instead of taking coffee each morning in order to wake up, try splashing cold water on your face. It is a healthier and more effective wake-up. Thereafter drink half a litre of water, the ultimate goal being 3 litres of water a day. Keep on having half litre drinks until you go to bed i.e. just before you lie down drink another half a litre. Water absorbs negativity.

PRINCIPLE #86: Self-Invest in Digital Personal Growth

Businesses invest over a billion dollars annually on research and development. May I ask you how much time and money you, as a person, are investing in your own research and development this year?

Let me give you the answer: not enough. Start with 30 dollars a month. You will find out how to escape to digital prosperity.

I

PRINCIPLE #87: Be 100% enthusiastic

Enthusiasm makes everything different through the Law of Attraction. You can´t control the length of each day, but you can control its impact by adding fun and enthusiasm. When you have enthusiasm for life, life has enthusiasm for you thanks to the Universe Laws. A smile is an asset ; a frown is a liabillity. Some people grin and bear it : others smile and change it. Smiling – being happy and enthusiastic – is always a choice, not a result. It improves your personality and peoples´opinion of you. Failure is a situation, never a person because leaders put themselves on top of circumstances. Therefore they turn it around with enthusiasm

PRINCIPLE #88: Take digital responsibility for your life

Almost all of us do not want to take digital responsibility for what is not working out well in our lives. To take responsibility, we have to admit we may have done something foolish or wrong.   Most of us don´t think much about behaviour, but if we did we would realize that all any human being does from birth to death is behave. Therefore, our ability to succeed digitally, as well as anything we attempt, depends on how well we learn to choose effective digital behaviours in the 4.0 World.

PRINCIPLE #89: Be a daily digital leader

Make every day count digitally starting with TODAY. Leadership is earned every day, it strengthens itself with time. Leadership is made to exercise it digitally. If leadership is followed by digitally results which the majority consider reasonable, leadership never decreases but increases with time and exponentially due to the power of digital networks.

PRINCIPLE #90: Develop financial intelligence in the digital world.

Financial intelligence is not so much how much money you make digitally but how much money you keep, how hard that money works for you, and how many generations (your children and the children of your children) you save it for.

PRINCIPLE #91: Seize the digital opportunity

Digital opportunities come our way in various forms and sizes and often they are disguised. Most opportunities are " slippery little suckers", as Julia Roberts said in the movie Pretty Woman. Most 2.0 digital opportunities came right at the time of a profound global crisis in 2008. Now it will be the same in the 4.0 world.

PRINCIPLE #92: Turn 1.0 failure into 2.0 digital success

Failure 1.0 is success 2.0 turned inside out. Failure is the digital bridge. Sure, some people stop in the middle of it and jump off, but others recognise that the digital bridge has a brand new plot of land at the other end. Just keep on walking digitally. Don´t be afraid if you find yourself on another digital bridge some day, and another, and another. They all lead somewhere. Keep going. The idea is not stop walking and, most importantly, to know where it is that you want to go digitally.

PRINCIPLE #93: Follow your digital course

" In whatever arena of life one may meet the challenge of courage, whatever may be the sacrifices he faces if he follows his conscience – the loss of his friends, his fortune, his contentment, even the esteem of his fellow men – each man must decide for himself the course he will follow". John F. Kennedy in his book Profiles in Courage. Apply this from Kennedy to the Digital World. You will soon realize that the courage of others will help you to follow suit. Success is closer than you think but certainly far from your living room sofa. Move on!

PRINCIPLE #94: Be a digital life player not a life fighter

Draw an enlargement of this principle and place it on your network digital wall. Just to keep from taking yourself too seriously, you might want to write somewhere on your chart **" Digital Business Angels fly because they take themselves lightly"**. I heard this long time ago, and it stills makes me smile because José Ballesteros de la Puerta reminds it to me regularly (Jorge the real angels protect you while you sleep). It constantly reminds me that you can drop an awful lot of excess baggage if you learn to play with life (creative state) instead of fighting it (competitive state).

PRINCIPLE #95: Read 1 hour a day

Reading is to the mind as exercise is to the body. This is true. And now easier in the digital age. Reading for an hour each day will translate into about one e-book per week. One e-book per week will translate into 50 books per year. Fifty e-books per year will translate into 500 books over the next 10 years. Since the average adult reads less than one book per year, when you begin reading one hour per day, one e-book per week, this alone will give you an incredible edge in your field. **You will become one of the smartest, most competent, and highest digital leaders in your profession by simply reading one hour each day and sharing your wisdom with your network like Ronald C.Stern does after reading 4000 books.**

PRINCIPLE #96: Defend free market economics

The US with Obama, Singapore and Spain, during the glorious days of José María Aznar, are three examples of countries where the free market policies have substantially reduced the level of poverty. Entrepreneurship works. Obama was quick enough to visit LinkedIn in Silicon Valley and have long talks with enthusiastic audiences.

PRINCIPLE #97: Your 3.0 business model is unique

The key to success in the 3.0 digital business world isn´t the lowest prices ; rather, it is finding a business model that works, and then working that model over and over again.

PRINCIPLE #98: Be an agent for digital change

My advice to you is hang in there to have digital success! People will doubt and people will obstruct. A certain amount of that may even be necessary. What I´ve found is that very often the people who oppose change are just cautious in the beginning. But once they buy in, they become your biggest supporters in your digital network. Trust your people. Stick to your guns and keep your dreams alive.

.

PRINCIPLE #99: Being digitally careful is better than fearful

Never be fearful digitally just be careful because careful is cerebral ; fearful is emotional.

Careful is fueled by digital information ; fearful is fueled by imagination, usually Lucifer driven. Careful calculates risk ; fearful avoids risks. Careful wants to achieve success ; fearful wants to avoid failure.

.

PRINCIPLE #100: Foster true Digital LinkedIN Group 2.0 thinking

Digital LinkedIN Groupthink bring new ideas, as ideas are not born in a conforming environment. Whenever people get together, there is the danger of groupthink. This is the phenomenon in which LinkedIN group members interact with each other. William Glasser did say that 95% of what we learn is from what we teach to others. The P2P world is proving this to bet rue.